PORTRAIT OF A DEPUTY PUBLIC DEFENDER

or, how I became a punk rock lawyer

JUANITA E. MANTZ, ESQ.

BAMBOO
DART
PRESS

LOS ANGELES † NEW YORK † LONDON † MELBOURNE

Portrait of a Deputy Public Defender by Juanita E. Mantz

ISBN: 978-1-947240-30-8

eISBN: 978-1-947240-31-5

An earlier version of the essay "A Re-Imagining" previously ran in *The Riverside Lawyer Magazine*

For information:

Bamboo Dart Press

chapbooks@bamboodartpress.com

Curated and operated by Dennis Callaci and Mark Givens

Bamboo Dart Press 012

Pelekinesis
www.pelekinesis.com

BAMBOO DART PRESS
www.bamboodartpress.com

SHRIMPER
www.shrimperrecords.com

For Adrian, my husband and soulmate, who loves punk/
post-punk music as much as I do.

And for my mom and dad who taught me how to
dream.

What people are saying about
Portrait of a Deputy Public Defender

What do the Talking Heads and the Clash have to do with the Post Conviction Justice Project Clinic at USC? Everything. Music is not just the soundtrack, but indeed the grounding inspiration for Juanita E. Mantz's depiction of her evolution from punk princess drop-out to deputy public defender in Riverside California. Mantz's hybrid memoir makes hard left turns and arrives at surprising destinations; after a toxic stop in corporate law (where one white male partner mistakes her for a paralegal), the author returns to California, rejects the big dollars and elects working with poor clients, many of whom are categorized as mentally incompetent. In dramatic anecdotes that read like stanzas of the Bowie/Mercury song "Under Pressure," Mantz describes the broken criminal system she must navigate, even as she follows an internal moral compass that never lets her or her readers off the hook. At moments raucous and at others deeply melancholy, *Portrait of a Deputy Public Defender* forces us to consider our past and our future: why bail doesn't work and how the murder of George Floyd challenges us to do more to transform the criminal justice system, and our relationship with each other. An irresistible, thoughtful, and inspiring read.

—**Stephanie Barbé Hammer**, author of *The Puppet Turners of Narrow Interior*, and *Rescue Plan*

There's nothing punk about being a lawyer unless you're a deputy public defender like Juanita E. Mantz. Mantz went from nearly "ruining her own life in just months" senior year to becoming a defender of mentally ill patients, representing those who have been found unfit to stand trial, rendered nearly voiceless by the system designed to protect them. From Mantz, we learn about the system from the inside, and how her own struggles and punk ethos brought her to this work.

—**Michelle Cruz Gonzales** author of *The Spitboy Rule: Tales of a Xicana in a Female Punk Band*

Mantz has put her record collection and big black boots where her mouth is in her work as a deputy public defender; every day she fights to help the poor and mentally ill, she embodies the music and lyrics of her favorite punk bands that kept her fired up as a teenage high school dropout. After reading this impassioned, deeply personal work that weaves memoir and poetry with the heartbreaking ins and outs of a broken legal system, I can think of no one else living their values as purely as she is.

—**Shawna-Lee I. Perrin**, author of *Radio Waves: A Post-Punk Novel*

Like the allegory of the twin brothers in her essay, "Bail - How Times Are A-Changin'," there are so many ways in which Juanita E. Mantz and I have led parallel lives. We are both Inland Empire Gen X'ers, Class of 1989. We both shoplifted and lived to tell about it. Listened to the same music. Got our butts kicked in fights we were sorely outmatched for. Skipped school. Wrote poetry. We were honors and GATE kids who lost their way. My own high school graduation hinged on my repeated failure of Algebra 1, but at the last minute, the counselors decided that my computer science class —yes, the one where we learned to make cheesy greeting cards with clip art and cliches—counted as math, barely squeaking by while I watched as my best friend became valedictorian.

But here is where our stories diverged: She did not graduate. And yet, because of that punk rock resistance to conform to expectations, she turned her failure to an advantage and determination, first getting her G.E.D., then a B.A. in English Lit, and her J.D. from USC. She ditched the lucrative world of corporate law to become a punk rock deputy public defender, using her experience as a troubled youth as a springboard for empathy and advocacy. And now, once a writer, always a writer, she's onward toward her MFA, and using her voice as a megaphone to call out the injustices she's witness to every day in the courtroom, advocating for those the system seeks to silence and sweep under the rug. These essays are proof that, "Tomorrow is another day. You will be OK." Especially for those in the criminal justice system who've got Juanita on their side.

—**Cati Porter**, author of *The Body at a Loss*, executive director of the Inlandia Institute

Through *Portrait of a Deputy Public Defender*, we are afforded the chance to witness the individuality, commitment and passion of one woman's vision. Juanita E. Mantz has an unfaltering strength rooted in a unique mestizaje: a Latina warrior heart and a punk rock passion for the marginalized, the abandoned and the voiceless. Her stories trace the faultlines of teen angst and the urgent lack of agency one feels when left alone, only to find a deep well of purpose aimed towards protecting the undefended. An illuminating account of the real battles from within the criminal justice system.

—**Leticia Del Toro**, author, *Café Colima*

In gentle and compassionate prose, Juanita E. Mantz pulls back the curtain on the criminal justice system in a way the general public does not ordinarily see, and places us squarely into the shoes of her clients whose humanity is above anything else. Revealing her own personal history as a high school dropout and her enduring love for punk rock, Mantz reveals her strength to rise as an attorney who does not give up on her clients, especially in our society which has normalized the "criminal" as someone to be discarded and forgotten. Mantz reveals an egregiously broken system where economic structures can doom the most economically vulnerable to criminality. Mantz's memoir as a Deputy Public Defender is a must-read for every American who cares about our justice system and the individuals who endure within it.

—**Elsa Valmidiano**, author of *We Are No Longer Babaylan*

This is for the fuckups, punks, Chicanas, and the working class kids who grew up thinking: the world wasn't made in my image. *Portrait of a Deputy Public Defender* is the defiant letter to a younger self you wish you had read when you were spiraling, and hadn't quite found yourself. Juanita does not speak in a whisper, or an affirmation. Instead, this chapbook spills the messiness of her life onto the page and teaches those of us who grew up in a broken system how to unbreak ourselves.

—**Michelle Villegas Threadgould**, journalist, poet, and author

Portrait of a Deputy Public Defender or, how I became a punk rock lawyer by Juanita E. Mantz is a rebel call for systematic change in a punitive society that blindly rips the heart out of our humanity every day while most of us go about our business unaware. From the trenches, Mantz pleads and demands that the already broken are given a second chance. She shares her own battles with mental illness and makes herself one with those who, because of their mental illness, have found themselves facing punishment and rejection instead of care. She does all of this while staying true to her working class upbringing and inner punk rock angst.

—**Emily Fernandez**, author of *Procession of Martyrs*

In this beautiful book, Juanita E. Mantz traces her journey from SoCal misfit and high school dropout to Houston corporate lawyer and eventually deputy public defender in Riverside County, where she now serves indigent and mentally ill clients. Every page shows readers that punk rock is a daily choice that transcends the haircut or black boots one may leave behind. With fierce honesty, conscience, and tenderness—both bruja and banshee—Mantz is the Gen-X fighter you will love to find on your side.

—**Jo Scott-Coe**, author of *MASS: A Sniper, a Father, and a Priest* (Pelekinesis)

"I will not serve that in which I no longer believe, whether it call itself my home, my fatherland, or my church: and I will try to express myself in some mode of life or art as freely as I can and as wholly as I can..."

James Joyce from *A Portrait of the Artist as a Young Man*

CONTENTS

How Did I Get Here?

It is 1989 and high school graduation day at Chaffey High School in Ontario, California. I know it is 1989 because Pizza Hut is still a restaurant, everyone walks around school with their Walkmans, and concert tickets are cheap and you still have to wait in a line at Music Plus to buy them.

1989 is the same year that The Cure releases *Disintegration*, the best album ever. When my best friend Tracy's parents leave town to go on bowling tournaments for the weekend, Tracy and I turn her CD player on full blast and dance for hours yelling out the lyrics to "Pictures of You," downing Coors Lite like it is water, which it kinda is.

It is thirty years later, and on the weekends, Tracy and I still do this but we've switched from CDs to vinyl and from Coors Lite to Michelob Ultras.

1989 is also the year I drop out of high school, five credits short of a diploma.

I am sitting in the bleachers with my mom, my dad, and my younger sister Annie. I am supposed to be graduating today with my twin sister Jackie and my best friend Tracy, but I threw it all away. This former straight A student went from goody two shoes to punk rock high school dropout. It only took me months to ruin my life.

My tío, Roland, who is a dead ringer for Wolfman Jack, is also here, down from Orange County. Roland will not look at me. I can sense his disappointment. I was always his favorite. When Jackie walks up in her graduation robe and cap, he says, "Congratulations, mija" in his gravelly voice and hugs her, handing her fifty dollars. I look up into the sky, blinking.

My mom won't look at me. She says I broke her heart by dropping out. My mom taught me and Jackie to read when we were three by sitting with us at our small kitchen table every day sounding out the words. My mom always said I was the smart one.

My dad puts his hand on my shoulder, but I push his hand away and go hide underneath the school's bleachers. The bleachers cover me in their shadow.

I think, how did I get here? I was supposed to go to Claremont McKenna. I was in all "gifted" classes, a member of the swim team and yearbook. I got good grades. School wasn't hard, life was. Instead of going to class senior year, I slept all day and drank all night.

The worst part is, I never really made the decision to drop out. It was just easier. I remember my mom saying there was no money for college. I had no idea about student loans. I just gave up. It was easier to sleep all day than try to make my way through the darkness. The truth is, I had been fighting depression for years and years. I grew up in chaos, with a lot of upheaval and fighting.

Things got even worse when my dad lost his bar and then the bank took the house during my junior year of high school. My parents would fight every night, their fights on repeat like the Smiths and X albums I would blast to drown it all out.

After they lost the house, we moved from rental to rental like nomads. There were bright points, ditching with my friends and concert after concert in Hollywood. But those moments were just an escape really.

Back under the bleachers, it smells like piss. I light up and tears drip on my cigarette. I wipe at my thick Siouxsie Sioux-lined eyes with the edge of my Sex Pistols tee. Music from the school's marching band echoes in my ears. I stare down at my monkey boots and tap my feet on the concrete thinking, I am a fucking loser. My life is over.

I think of being at the Hollywood Palladium seeing The Smiths and how I danced and screamed with joy when Morrissey took the stage.

When Jackie's name is called, I flinch and I know that I can't watch her walk. Look, I know that I should go out into the sun and watch her graduate. I know I should be happy for her, she's my wonder twin. My mom always said we had our own language as kids. At least one of us made it. But I can't be happy, and bury my head in my arms.

I am not a cool punk rock girl anymore, it was all just an act. Sobbing, it's all coming out of me, like water from a broken tap.

As I stare down at the concrete beneath my feet, I think back to sitting at the park when I was little and how I would always wonder, is everyone's life like this?

I always took a book to the park when my mom kicked us out of the house, when my parents fought, which was often. I thought about all the books I would read, some of them by flashlight, and how I would squint into them and lose myself. I read *Gone with the Wind*, F. Scott Fitzgerald, Judy Blume, SE Hinton and of course, my mom's Harlequin romance novels.

Those books meant everything to me. They saved me and showed me the possibilities of life. Then later, in high school, I found punk and post-punk music and was saved again.

There was something in punk rock anarchy and the dark wave of post-punk that touched my very soul and showed me I was not all alone in the world, that there was life after darkness. Music was a place I could go to be with all of my sadness.

The lyrics to my favorite song by The Smiths whispers in my head. "And if a double decker bus crashes into us, to die by your side, is such a heavenly way to die."

Did I want to die?

I wipe at my face and shake my head. I decide at that moment, under those stinky bleachers, that I want to live. That I want out of this pissant town and want to prove myself to everyone who gave up on me. I think, all is not lost, I just need a plan. I could take my GED and go back to college. I tell myself, you will be

OK. Tomorrow is another day.

Tomorrow was another day, and there were many more days. I worked and worked, and it took years and years. My journey was not a straight path. I took the GED the summer after I dropped out and passed it easily. All my honors classes had paid off. I started waitressing and when I saved enough, I moved into an apartment and relished the quiet. My little sister Annie moved in with me and I enrolled in junior college part-time. I ran the school newspaper. It was hard going with no reliable car, walking to work, and begging for rides to school. But I made it work.

It took me years and years to transfer to UCR, but once I finally transferred, I graduated magna cum laude from UCR in two years with an English literature degree. I applied to law school on a lark. When the large envelope came in the mail from USC Law, I knew my life was changing forever. That I would be OK.

Almost two decades ago, I graduated from USC Law wearing a cardinal and gold cap and gown. My parents were in the audience beaming. My sisters and my best friend Tracy waved at me with huge smiles. No longer was I that sad, high school dropout hiding under the bleachers. I had made it.

After a detour into corporate law, I found my destiny as a deputy public defender, one who represents the most mentally ill in Riverside, California. I've been doing this work for over a decade and will probably do it at least a decade more. Whenever I feel it is too much—too sad and too traumatic—I think, my clients need me. That need is everything. It gives me purpose,

Ironically enough, being a high school dropout is my magic wand. My history is what makes me a great deputy public defender. I have been where my clients are, hopeless and sad. I have had no car, no money, and no hope. But, I made it out.

Recently, I represented one of the saddest clients of my career. Many people would have given up. Yet, my persistence and visualization for my client made a miracle happen. There are few happy endings in my line of work, but I saved this client from prison and the client will be in a safe place.

My clients are all in dire situations, but no matter what their circumstances are, I always try and give them hope. I tell my clients what I told myself that day underneath the bleachers so long ago.

Tomorrow is another day. You will be OK.

STATIC

Can you hear me?
Screaming in my head
Let my people go
Let me go

Saying let us go
Release everyone
From this system
That hurts us all

As a deputy public defender
I used to think
I could work within it
Now I see it's broken

Can you hear me?
Screaming in your ear
Listen to me
Please listen, listen!

Let me do what I do
Then let me go
From this misery
Of banging my head

My ears are ringing
From the beat of cuffs
On bars of cells
Across America

Are you there?
Can you hear me?
Screaming your name
It all still remains

Excuse me
Excuse you
Forgive me
Forgive us all

We know not what we do
Or maybe we do

Changing the World

Sometimes, you must work within a broken system with broken people. That is my job as a deputy public defender representing the incompetent to stand trial. My clients are the most voiceless and powerless. Many of my clients have no family support. I am their one lifeline to justice and often the only source for advocacy for their mental health and cognitive issues.

My clients have allegedly committed a wide range of alleged crimes, from petty theft crimes and disobeying court orders to felonies that range anywhere from vandalism to criminal threats to murder. The majority of my clients are pretrial, meaning most have not been convicted of anything at all.

Once an attorney declares a doubt as to a person's competence to stand trial, my goal is to lead my clients through a strained and broken system with integrity and grace, treating them as I would wish my own family members to be treated. They deserve that respect. The machinery of the criminal system, as well as the civil commitment system that I work within, is a terrifying one and I try and make it less chaotic for my clients.

Although they often do not understand what is happening to them, they do know, I hope, that I care desperately for them and for their rights and that I will fight with all of my will for their protection. For the ones with family, I always keep in mind who I represent, i.e., the client, because I have to do what's in the best legal interest of the individual I represent, which can conflict with the family's interest.

As the Talking Heads once asked, how did I get here? I worked in the USC Post Conviction Justice Project clinic as a student supervisor when I was a student at USC Law.

While there, I represented a battered woman who had received a life sentence for watching her abusive husband murder someone. After years of work on her case—which I only did a portion of under the supervision of the clinical professors—our clinic, finally, had her released from Chino State Prison. She had been shackled during her trial in Riverside which is patently unconstitutional and the challenging by our office resulted in a vacating of her conviction and her eventual release more than a decade after her original conviction.

That law school experience taught me how important it is to have a zealous lawyer on a case and how very much the role matters to the most oppressed and powerless in our society.

Despite that experience, I chose big firm life as my first career and ended up in Houston at the largest law firm representing Shell Oil. My only excuse is that I had been working class and bill poor my whole life and wanted out, especially out of the small Southern California town that I grew up in.

What I found, however, was a soul-sapping existence representing corporations and within six years, I had decided enough was enough. I came back to my hometown in the Inland

Empire region of Southern California and eventually was hired in Riverside as a deputy public defender, coming full circle.

The day I started as a deputy public defender was like the day I wrote my first story. I knew it was meant to be and that I was meant to do the work.

The nuts and bolts of the incompetency proceedings are this: people can be incompetent to stand trial due to mental illness, developmental disabilities, and cognition disorders.[1] Mental illness can be treated while cognitive and developmental disabilities are static and for the most part, they do not change. The percentage of those with mental illness in the "system" has been reported at close to 50 percent.[2]

I believe it may even be higher.

Maybe because I cannot have children, I feel an overwhelming protectiveness toward all of my clients. It is maternal. Plus, as a person who struggled with depression in high school and after law school, I always think, but for the grace of a higher power, go all of us.

---

[1] This area of the law is governed by state statute and related case law. See California Penal Code Section 1367 et seq. and CALCRIM No. 3451. Present Mental Competence of Defendant (Judicial Council of California Criminal Jury Instructions).

[2] "Report urges Riverside County to focus on mental health care, not jails", *The Press Enterprise* by Jeff Horseman, April 5, 2017.

Mental illness does not know race or privilege. It strikes everywhere, but the poor have fewer resources and end up in this broken system. It is so unfair as well as patently discriminatory and traumatic for my clients who end up in cages for years. Many of my clients already carry childhood trauma in addition to being mentally ill, poor, and lacking a support system. My clients languish in the jails in a small cell awaiting treatment which often makes their illness worse. But there is nowhere for them to go, and our criminal system does not care that they are pretrial and have not been found guilty of anything.

Perhaps, if we had community placements, instead of in-custody incarceration and interment, clients might be able to restore ("restore" meaning to get better to the point they can handle their criminal case) without any hospitalization. Yet there are few community placements[3] and my clients cannot afford bail.

---

[3] Community placements for the mentally ill (when they cannot live at home) typically consists of board and care housing where the house manager takes the clients to their mental health appointments. Another placement is residential rehabilitation, which typically focuses on addiction rather than mental health wellness. Unfortunately, most board and care placements are overwhelmed and underfunded and many residential rehabilitations do not have the infrastructure to support clients with severe mental health issues. The thing that is desperately needed is large scale housing for the mentally ill. We need housing that treats my clients' variety of issues holistically, which typically include mental health as well as physical health and wellness, along with treating their trauma and addiction issues.

My goal in representing this population is to change this placement issue. The truth is, we need beds. People need a place to go where they can get well. Jail is not the answer. Let me repeat that, jail is not the answer. It only creates more problems.

Back to semantics, my goal is to always help my clients get treatment so they can be restored to stand trial. But not everyone is restorable, especially those with very severe mental illness, and/or developmental and cognitive disabilities. When clients do restore, their cases are reinstated (proceedings are suspended during the process) and they can resolve their cases. I often refer them to our sister program, mental health court, or mental health diversion.

What people need to understand is this: my clients can be held for two years on a felony (it used to be three years in California, but recently the law changed) and one year on a misdemeanor, without good time credit[4]. My clients often do way more time than they would if they were competent to stand trial and were able to resolve their cases. The injustice of this is palpable, especially when jail is a dangerous place health-wise (which we all realize, I hope, post-pandemic) and the mentally ill and developmentally disabled are at high risk for becoming victims themselves.

Ultimately, if found incompetent, my clients are held in the state hospital, but the wait list is months long. Many misdemeanor

---

[4] Most people incarcerated in the county jail receive day-for-day credit on any future plea, meaning if someone spends 30 days in custody, they will get 60 days of credit toward their sentence.

clients never get any treatment at all, and instead just spend their time in a cell in the jail awaiting a bed that never materializes in time and then are released to fend for themselves. It often seems like an exercise in futility.

For a useful discussion of the way the mentally ill are treated in America, *Insane: America's Criminal Treatment of Mental Illness* by Alisa Roth illustrates just how cruel our system of incarceration is. Roth describes a client who blinded himself in jail when he should have been hospitalized instead of arrested. I have had clients who mutilated themselves in custody. I know those clients. I have represented those clients. Many clients are sick and made sicker by a cruel system of injustice.

A couple of clients come to mind.[5] I recall an older woman who was charged with drug sales. Her exposure was over fifteen years due to her drug sales convictions/priors which adds an additional three years of criminal exposure for every sales "prior" conviction[6]. The case was years old as the complaint was filed at the tale end of the statute of limitations. When she came to court, the client was disheveled and confused. She kept asking the deputy to let her out so she could go feed her cat. She did not know where she was. It turns out, the client had dementia, early onset as she was in her late fifties. When I spoke with her son, I learned that she had been deteriorating cognitively for years. It took me almost

---

[5] Details have been changed to preserve client autonomy.

[6] See California Health and Safety Code Section 11370.2.

two years to show that this client could never be restored. She could never understand what was going on. Toward the end of her multiple years of incarceration, she was at serious risk in the jail and would bang her head against the wall. I eventually was able to get her cases dismissed and move her to a care facility, but it took way too long. That woman and her predicament still haunts me to this day.

Another client who comes to mind is someone I met many years ago when I first started practicing incompetency law. He was elderly and had burned his house down in the throes of a schizophrenic delusion and his older sister, who was in her seventies, died of smoke inhalation. The client was also intellectually disabled and deaf, having had a serious illness as a child. The client was charged with arson and with the murder of his sister. In my opinion, the case was, at its heart, an accidental or negligent fire setting, not an intentional murder or a malicious arson.

The client was extremely impaired but could parrot certain things if it was repeated to him over and over. We fought this case for years. The client lingered in the jail, shuffling back and fourth between jail and the state hospital. After hiring our own cognition expert, I was able to prove that he was so cognitively and intellectually disabled and mentally ill that he could not assist counsel. The state hospital kept sending him back saying he was better and restored to competency and that he could understand and assist. I took the case to trial numerous times until, ultimately, at the last trial on his incompetency, he was deemed permanently incompetent and moved to a conservatorship. This is a client that the prosecution was seeking prison on and a client that they threatened to charge with the death penalty. The prosecution wanted life in prison for this severely impaired and disabled client who had little or no understanding, or even culpability. Ultimately, we saved that client from a torturous existence in prison, a place where he would not have survived.

Despite all of the hurdles and heartbreaks, it is a gift to do this work. To be able to represent my clientele is a privilege. What I do is very complicated and intense, involving constitutional, civil, and criminal complexities that it has taken me years and years to become an expert in.

I fight forced medication orders because no client deserves to be held down and forced to take medication against their will. If you force them, they will never want to take medication. Many of the psychotropic medications have severe side effects that can damage kidneys and nervous systems. Medications are highly beneficial to most of my clientele, but everyone should have body autonomy.

My days in court (what we call being "on calendar") are exhausting. I typically have ten to twenty clients on calendar and I must be efficient in court because my clients have little tolerance for the courtroom environment. I also do trial work, which allows me to put my storytelling skills to good use in the courtroom. My favorite part of my job is telling my client's stories in an attempt to persuade and educate others with privilege and power about the role mental illness plays in the criminal system, in an attempt to undermine the stigma surrounding mental illness.

Now, after more than a decade of doing this work, I struggle with whether I am perpetuating a broken system. Lately, I have begun to wonder whether I should be addressing the crisis on a macro-level with my writing and advocacy, rather than with the micro-level work I do as a lawyer where I am trying to help one client at a time.

Last year, in an article for *Aljazeera*, I wrote about how the Covid-19 pandemic demonstrated to me just how very invisible and at risk my incarcerated clients are.[7] As a nation, the United States is incarcerating millions of people in jails and state hospitals, often with substandard medical care.[8] The pandemic has put my clients' lives even more at risk.[9]

I could say that no one cares, but that's not true. I care, along with many others, but we are all overwhelmed and stymied by the

---

[7] US prisons are woefully unequipped to deal with coronavirus, *Aljazeera* by Juanita E. Mantz, March 12, 2020.

[8] "Mass Incarceration: The Whole Pie 2020", *The Prison Policy Initiative* by Wendy Sawyer and Peter Wagner, Match 24, 2020; "California's jails are so bad some inmates beg to go to prison instead", *LA Times* by Abbie Vansickle and Manuel Villa, May 23, 2019.

[9] "Fateful choices as coronavirus raged through Riverside jail hitting deputies and inmates", *LA Times* by Alene Tchekmedyian and Kailyn Brown, April 27, 2020; "Sick inmates and their advocates fear deadly coronavirus infections", *The Press Enterprise* by Brian Rokos, May 15, 2020.

massive change that would be needed to change mass incarceration policies and the stigma against the mentally ill.

My clients need me so desperately, that in the end, I have decided to stay, and keep fighting the good fight every day. But now I call myself an abolitionist and not a reformer. I will continue to fight to change the system from the inside, but now I want huge systemic and foundational changes.

The question that remains is whether the people with the power, the prosecutors, can change. If the prosecutors see people as bad and have had to dehumanize them to do what they do, how do they ever change? Maybe, put a public defender as a head of the prosecution's office and see what happens. Maybe elect someone progressive who wants to truly enact change. Some jurisdictions like Los Angeles, who recently elected a progressive prosecutor named George Gascón, are doing just that.

In short, clean house.

Things will change when you lead with empathy. This essay does not focus on the racial and economic component, but suffice to say, most of my incarcerated clients are indigent and black or brown and/or poor white folk. Many started in the state foster care system and/or dependency system, and/or were abandoned by their families for being mentally ill or developmentally disabled. Many of my client's own parents were incarcerated and/or have mental illness. My clients are most often the recipients of generations of trauma. This is trauma that we are perpetuating, trauma that will last, and has lasted, generations.

Some of my clients have very loving supportive families, families that just need more support and services, and this support is often hard to find or simply does not exist in the community unless you have a criminal case. For them, this system is maddening.

Lately, I have learned and vowed to trust my voice, to say the hard things that need to be said. That is the only way any of this will ever change.

Change is the only thing that will help my clients. Real change will probably only come with a global and generational shift in thinking. True change will also only come when society sees my clients the way I see them—as people to be saved rather than imprisoned. We should be seeking salvation, not incarceration.

For as the late, great David Bowie once said, "These children that you spit on, as they try and change their worlds, are immune to your consultations, they're quite aware what they are going through."

A Metamorphosis

"I cannot make you understand. I cannot make anyone
understand what is happening inside me.
I cannot even explain it to myself."

Franz Kafka, *The Metamorphosis*

In my sophomore year of high school, my metamorphosis
began. I gave up being a goody-goody and ditched the swim
team, along with school most days, and dyed my hair blue/black.
Soon after, I pierced my nose which was shocking to many at my
high school back in the 1980s. I began wearing all black outfits
to school paired with combat boots, an ankh necklace and thick
black eyeliner mimicking the eyes of Siouxsie Sioux, my favorite
singer from the band Siouxsie and the Banshees.

By junior year, the change was complete. The new style got me
attention. I would walk the quad with my best friends, Tracy and
Melinda, all decked out in black, and sometimes we could hear
whispers. "They'll put a spell on you."

With eager hand wringing curiosity, we bought a book on
Wicca and pledged to only do white magic. But in truth, the
only magic we really attempted was reading our fortunes with
tarot cards and poring over horoscopes and astrology books at the
Crystal Cave in Claremont. We were a three member coven, one
without any spells, potions, or powers.

In truth, I was more of a poser Catholic Mexican witch who was more style than substance, one who was really into the dark wave music by bands like The Cure, Joy Division, The Smiths, and Sisters of Mercy along with punk bands like The Sex Pistols, The Clash, Generation X, The Ramones, The Buzzcocks, and my favorite Los Angeles punk band X.

My Mexican mom was horrified by my change in style and would say disdainfully, "You look like a bruja, a witch, so ridiculous, why do you dress like that?" My tías said, "Que fea! That's so ugly, Mija. Take off those combat boots." My white cowboy dad was more gentle and would say, "Jenny, don't dye your hair so dark, it's so much prettier brown."

What no one understood however, was that my change from goody two shoes to goth-like punk princess, was not about my outside. It was about my insides. It was interior not exterior, the change I mean. I recognized way back then, although I was never educated about it until years later, that I had a melancholy sensibility.

Add in a punk rock recipe for anarchy and bucking the system and my change to a punk rock girl was predestined in my soul. When I found the art (namely, punk and dark wave music) that touched off a creative spark waiting to be lit in me, there was no going back.

Homecoming, in my mom's opinion, was a disaster from the pictures. My mom didn't appreciate my date's mohawk or my shiny iridescent black dress with lace sleeves that would make any goth girl swoon. She hated my blue black hair curled in waves and my stud earring in one nostril. And my makeup! Black eyeliner lined so thick on the upper lid that it would take days to come off. And bright red lipstick in a cupid bow.

My mom wailed, "Oh no, how can I show these pictures to my relatives and friends?"

Instead of bowing my head, I should have looked her in the eye and responded, "I am, and will always remain, inside and sometimes out, a punk rock girl."

A Re-Imagining

As I sit here after enduring the pandemic, I think to myself, humans are an adaptable species. Perhaps that is our weakness. We cannot always see danger, even when it is in our faces or sits on our chests. We adapt to circumstances without even realizing the scariness of the situation.

When I first became a deputy public defender more than a decade ago, after years in corporate litigation, I adapted too. At first, I was horrified by all of the people in custody and then, like most of us who work within the criminal system day in and day out, I became somewhat desensitized. That's not to say I stopped caring. I have always cared so much that it hurt. But, somehow, even my empathetic soul stopped being shocked by the mass incarceration and subjugation of so many human beings. I stopped being shocked by double digit offers from the Prosecution, offers that I have a duty to relay to my clients. Prosecutors would routinely ask my clients to plead to long prison sentences of ten to fifteen years, while also implying they would get even more time should said client take it to trial. That's a hell of an offer, especially when I believed these clients deserved probation not prison. I stopped being shocked by the abandonment of so many of the mentally ill to the streets and jails. I became accustomed to seeing police reports where an officer charges a mentally ill person in the throes of a delusion with a felony resisting arrest and/or criminal threats. I stopped being shocked by the subjugation of so very many people of color, poor people and the mentally ill and disabled.

Last year, that changed for many of us with the killing of George Floyd. The dam finally broke for many of us and I said, no more. Many of us prayed in our heads I am sure for something to finally change. We all pledged to do more.

Have we done more? Ask yourself, have we?

When we deputy public defenders collectively marched for George Floyd, in what feels like eons ago in this pandemic-tinged world, it felt hopeful. On that day, it felt as if things were finally changing. People were finally speaking up. Things that had been unsaid for far too long were being shouted.

As professor Angela Davis, who is one of the most prolific scholars on these issues, writes so eloquently in her book *Are Prisons Obsolete?*[10]

> "What would it mean to imagine a system in which punishment is not allowed to become the source of corporate profit? How can we imagine a society in which race and class are not determinative of punishment? Or one in which punishment itself is not the central concern in the making of justice."

What it would mean to imagine a new "system" is for us to think of criminal justice differently and look at it in a reimagined way to try and truly help people rather than hurt them. It means to try

---

10 *Are Prisons Obsolete?* by Angela Y. Davis, Seven Stories Press (2003).

and lift people up rather than harm them. It means removing our blinders so we can see that this criminal injustice system hampers people and ultimately destroys them. It treats them as "other" and harms us all in the process.

Ultimately, this system elevates punishment and retribution rather than rehabilitation and recovery. It creates roadblocks and barriers for those in the system trying to lead a healthy and productive life rather than assisting people to do well. A reimagining would mean making incarceration the last resort, not the first.

Remember too that all law is relative. Let me give you an example: When I started as a defense attorney in 2009, all drug offenses in Riverside were typically charged as felonies regardless of amount, especially methamphetamine. Marijuana cases were also commonly charged and at times, marijuana sales (a felony) was charged depending on the weight of the weed.

Yet, now, magically, all drug offenses for personal use (unless there are sales quantities) are charged as misdemeanors due to the advent of legislation in California mandating that these drug charges be misdemeanors. Marijuana is now legal.

What has changed? Have the drugs changed? No, of course not. If anything weed is stronger, but our public perception and attitudes regarding drug use and addiction have changed. Most importantly, drug laws have changed.

For years, before the laws changed, I would watch clients plead guilty over and over to prison for small quantities of drugs.

Prosecutors charged these cases zealously, enforcing what we know now to be an unjust law.

These same prosecutors, along with the police, will continue to enforce and charge whatever the law allows them to. Cops and prosecutors will go as far as we let them go. If pointing in the air was a crime, law enforcement would probably feel justified to charge it. Perhaps the problem is that these police and prosecutors are taught not to question the laws they enforce. I would argue that it is a moral imperative to use one's discretion.

Justice, however, should not be relative. Higher truths remain the same. What's right remains the same. Philosophically, social justice movements are born out of higher truths, out of the non-relative, out of a deeper knowledge and truth that we human beings all have in our bones.

History has shown us that prosecutors are not the ones who will lead the charge to a more just system or to a reimagining of a system. As I said above, these prosecutors will enforce whatever laws are on the books and do as they are told for the most part. Prosecutors are not rebels or warriors for justice in any sense of the word. They are metaphoric lemmings, leading our clients off a cliff, over and over. That is not to say there are no good prosecutors because there are good ones that try to do the right thing, but even their hands are tied in this cruel system of injustice.

Ask yourself, why is putting a human being in a cage so easy for this system? Where is the caring? Where is the love for our fellow humans?

Riverside County, where I work, still lags behind in progressive policies aimed at helping to end the subjugation and mass incarceration of people of color and poor folk. But, less than 100 miles away, Los Angeles has elected a new District Attorney, George Gascón[11], who, with a stroke of his justice pen, ended cash bail for all but serious felonies, and pledged to end most sentencing enhancements while also putting an end to juveniles being tried as adults. Will he succeed in changing this entrenched system of mass incarceration and injustice? We shall see.

Why should bail and incarceration depend on your California ZIP code? Thankfully, it may not anymore.

The California Supreme Court just addressed this very issue in a landmark case called *In re Kenneth Humphrey* holding that pretrial incarceration bail for the indigent, which has been the status quo for decades, is unconstitutional if there are less restrictive means to ensure public safety and client's attendance at court.[12]

I will discuss this in more detail later, but this ruling is a huge game changer for criminal justice. With regard to bail, we are

---

[11] New Los Angeles DA announces end to cash bail, the death penalty and trying children as adults", *CNN* by Alexandra Meeks and Madeline Holcombe, December 8, 2020.

[12] IN THE SUPREME COURT OF CALIFORNIA, *In re KENNETH HUMPHREY on Habeas Corpus,* S247278 First Appellate District, Division Two A152056 San Francisco City and County Superior Court 17007715, March 25, 2021.

almost always talking about incarceration pretrial and this is while you're still presumed innocent under the law. There is still a presumption of innocence in America but our bail policies would suggest otherwise.

As the *In Re Humphrey* case points out, at any given time, almost half a million people are in jail throughout the United States awaiting trial and they have not been convicted of anything yet. Pandemic or not, they're still incarcerating many, many people who deserve to be out of custody fighting their cases. This is not just a California issue, it is a national problem and an American problem of our own making.

Call it what it is. Say the truth. Economic disadvantage (in other words, being poor) impacts guilt or innocence through coercion. Every deputy public defender knows all too well that innocent people plead to get out of jail. It is the ultimate act of state coercion.

Ask yourself, most especially in pandemic times, wouldn't you have pleaded guilty if you could get out of jail? I would have in an instant.

As the rates of Covid-19 skyrocketed in California during the pandemic, the prisons, jails and state hospitals were severely impacted and those incarcerated were suffering and dying. Yet, there was silence in the face of an emergency, deafening silence.

I am not surprised. Due to adaptation we have all been complicit in the creation of an unfair, unjust, and dangerous criminal system. But I, for one, will be complicit no more.

No more adaptation. It is time for real change.

And a true reimagining.

HOW PUNK ROCK AND PUBLIC DEFENSE ALIGN

In high school, I was obsessed with Sid Vicious. His poster was tacked up on my bedroom wall and I would blow him a kiss before school every morning. Of course, I knew he was dead, but still, I fantasized about meeting him with his black leather jacket and spiky hair, a bass guitar in his hand and a dog collar around his neck.

My best friend Tracy and I would watch the movie *Sid and Nancy* obsessively. The couple seemed so tragic, like Romeo and Juliet, albeit a punk rock version. Some nights, I would dream of living back in the 1970's UK, which didn't seem so far away back then in the late '80s when I grew up. Sid's story fascinated my teenage self. He grew up poor and taught himself to play bass. He was a stylish clotheshorse, and didn't give a shit about anything it seemed.

As an adult, I must acknowledge that his true story is the opposite of romantic. It's sad, hopeless, and tragic despite his fame. His story, along with Nancy Spungen's, was more about addiction, mental health issues and sadly, his story ended up being about overdosing, murder, and suicide. But back then, I felt inspired by Sid's "I don't give a fuck" attitude.

Looking back, that's what got me most about punk music.

There was something in the freedom of punk—the anarchy and the rejection of strict social systems—that drew me in, along with the fashion, which I was always fascinated by.

As a young adult, I always loved me a guy with a mohawk and I can see myself in my mind's eye all gussied up in my ripped up tights, soled in the hard and utilitarian nature of combat boots or the Frankenstein thick aesthetic of Creepers. As a teenager, I commonly paired boxers over thermals and a punk tee with a thrift store oversized vest and blazer. The DIY of it all was compelling.

Kids in high school would ask me, why don't you listen to Power 106 (which was the Latinx dance music station). I would look at them askance, wondering why they were trying to fit me into a box. I listened to KROQ and the indie station in Claremont. I didn't feel constrained by my white and Latinx heritage to choose to be anything but me. Back then in the '80s, I didn't know of Latinx LA punk icons like Alice Bag who broke the gender and racial ceilings of punk. I would find out about her history later as an adult. Recently, I devoured her memoir *Violence Girl* which chronicles her childhood and rise in the LA punk scene.

What is punk for me? Punk means no rules and/or the breaking of rules, rebellion, no boundaries, inclusivity (at least it started that way) and a blue collar "fuck the man" ethos. Punk for me started with proto-punk bands like The New York Dolls, one of my favorite bands, who shattered gender norms by dressing in high heels, scarves, and makeup. People like Patti Smith, who was more of a poet than a punker really, but she was one of my heroines in high school. I devoured her album *Horses* and would learn that she was in the New York punk scene from the beginning and merged poetry and music in a new and novel way. And of course, there would be no punk without the incomparable chameleon, and my hero, David Bowie.

One of my favorite bands was, and is, the LA punk band X. There is something about the chaos of the punk and cowboy harmonies of John Doe and Exene Cervenka that always touched me. Of course, the Sex Pistols sparked something in my creative brain and let something loose inside of me. The Sex Pistols started it all for me, really, along with another "starter" band, The Ramones. There were other bands I loved, like Generation X with a young Billy Idol, and the Buzzcocks, which might sound like pop punk today, and The Replacements (Paul Westerberg's lyrics are sublime), along with dark wave and post-punk bands like Bauhaus, Joy Division, Siouxsie and the Banshees, The Cure, The Pixies, and The Smiths. As a teenager in the '80s, at least where I grew up in the Inland Empire, there was not much distinction between goth and punk, and the same kids who loved the Sex Pistols loved bands like Bauhaus, Joy Division, and Love and Rockets.

But there was also a political side to punk that drew me in, even as a teenager who was struggling to find herself and her voice. In high school and college, I would see people of color in my neighborhood pulled over and harassed, and knew that the police were not a benevolent force. The Clash speaks to this when they sing, "Police and thieves in the streets/Scaring the nation with their guns and ammunition." The song, in retrospect, can be seen as a prophecy about America's turn toward police militarization[13]. Likewise, Johnny Cash, who influenced punk bands like Social Distortion, sang at Folsom Prison and wrote songs that spoke to an unjust and harsh criminal system and world, something Cash was aware of firsthand due to his drug use and own incarceration and interactions with police, prosecutors, and the judiciary.

From a young age, I'd always had an innate sense of justice and strong empathy for the underdog. I would look at my mom toiling away, waitressing by day and spending her nights on the graveyard shift at Circle K, and think that's not fair. My mom was always wicked smart and could read a book in a day, yet she was constrained by time and circumstances having left school as a teenager after her mom died. My mom got her GED in her thirties. My dad was similarly constrained by his birthplace in post-depression Great Falls, Montana, having spent time in an orphanage for a while. He grew up so poor that the sight of rice would make him gag because that's all he ate for a time. Being

---

13 The song "Police and Thieves" was, interestingly enough, written by reggae artist Junior Murvin in 1976 and covered by the Clash a year later and included on their debut album. See "Culture Clash: Bob Marley, Joe Strummer and the punky reggae party", *The Guardian Music Blog*, September 19, 2014.

a truck driver was my dad's occupation which transitioned into moving furniture which broke him physically.

Yet still, my dad taught me to dream by accomplishing his biggest dream, owning a bar—which is so punk rock. His tavern, The Big O, only lasted a few years, but it was all his while it lasted. He put Joan Jett and the Go-Go's on the jukebox for us, both of whom started out in the punk scene (Joan Jett in her band The Runaways and Belinda Carlisle in the Germs). As kids, my sisters and I would go to the bar to help my dad clean and spend our early morning on the weekends and dance there, plugging the jukebox with quarters. As my mom always said, a drinker owning a bar is a disaster waiting to happen, and the disaster happened.

Dad had his dream and then a few years in, the bar was gone, as well as our house and any financial stability my family had.

A blue collar aesthetic is at the heart of all of this. As the Chicana writer and activist Cherríe Moraga has said, much more eloquently than I ever could, there is a language to the blue collar aesthetic.[14] In my memoir and childhood stories about growing up blue collar, I write in that language. Punks sing in that language. Public defenders fight in this language. The criminal system is very much about class and economics—starting with selective enforcement, and then bail, then moving to representation, and

---

14 "Voices of Feminism Oral History Project: Cherríe Moraga interviewed by Kelly Anderson", *Sophia Smith Collection*, Smith College Northampton, MA, June 6 & 7, 2005 in Oakland, California.

then to gang enhancements[15] and the imposition of the death penalty.

In most ways, the criminal system we have created in this country is anti-lower class which creates a sub class below lower and working class which I would call the "incarcerated class," people who are, in fact, incarcerated due to lack of economic privilege pretrial, people who would otherwise be free to fight their case on the outside except for the fact that they are poor.

What is most disturbing of all of this, is that the statistics and studies show that people's outcomes are worse if they have to fight the case while incarcerated.[16]

It makes sense. Someone who is in custody has fewer resources to draw on. They may feel pressure to rush the case to trial. My clients lose everything while incarcerated—their cars get impounded and sold, they lose their apartments, their benefits and even sometimes, their families.

---

[15] Gang enhancements are where a person is penalized by a Prosecutor adding the gang enhancement allegation, at times with little proof, of a person's active membership within a "gang" which results in "enhancing" any sentence by potentially adding additional years (and years) in prison if they are convicted of the felony and the enhancement. See California Penal Code 186.22(b).

[16] "The Downstream Consequences of Misdemeanor Pretrial Detention" (2017) 69 Stan. L.Rev 711, 759–769 by Paul Heaton, Sandra G. Mayson and Megan T. Stevenson; "The Hidden Costs of Pretrial Detention" by Christopher T. Lowenkamp, Ph.D., Marie Vannostrand Ph.D., and Alexander Holsinger, Ph.D., (November 2013).

In my work, I advocate for clients with no means. Every single one of our clients is poor, what the court system calls indigent, which is even below poor in a way. The vast majority are incarcerated. In my opinion, it's like this because they are the clients people want to throw away and punish and at best, forget. Out of sight, out of mind.

Public defense is the opposite of where I was after graduation from USC Law School. If public defense is McDonald's, corporate law litigation is Ruth's Chris Steak House. The only thing was, I hated big firm life. It was boring and tedious and hierarchical. Every motion had to be run up the pole of partners. There was no autonomy, I was a suit, a sell-out.

When I was an associate at the largest law firm in Houston, I didn't listen to music much. I certainly never did my eyeliner like Siouxsie Sioux or wore my combat boots. I told almost no one that I had dropped out of high school. Almost no one knew my father was a truck driver and my mom a waitress. I denied myself and my creative soul and I plunged into a deep depression. It all felt so wrong. I had become Eliza Doolittle and was paying the price for selling my soul. The firm was a very white shoe law firm with an occasional cowboy boot. I was put into torts even though my first choice was pure corporate law doing "deals", i.e., mergers. Later I saw that almost everyone in pure corporate law was a guy. With my love of editing, I may have missed my calling as that field is about reading/revising contracts all day.

There is one day that I remember vividly. I was a second-year associate and working on a large land use case over submerged property. The case took over my life. I did so much research that I didn't sleep for a week and walked into court excited to share it. Our co-counsel, an older white man from another Houston law firm who I had only communicated with via email, stopped me as I walked to the counsel table. He said, "Juanita, you're a paralegal, you're not allowed behind the bar."

"Paralegal?" I said with a questioning lilt to my voice. At first, I was shocked and confused. My face turned red when I realized he had assumed I was a paralegal and not a lawyer. I had been corresponding with him via email for weeks and weeks about the case.

"I am an attorney," I told him with a hard shake of my head and a deep frown. He stammered and apologized. I cried that night and when I asked the white partner that I worked for if there was anything I could have done differently, he shook his head and said kindly, "It's not you, it's him. You did everything perfect." Yet, despite his assurances, the experience stuck with me. I never felt as if I were enough.

After three years, I took the California bar and moved to join my long time boyfriend (now husband) who was attending dental school in San Francisco. My San Francisco law firm experience was similar to my experience in Texas. Different circus, but the same clowns. Somehow, I never felt the corporate litigation world accepted me. Or truth be told, maybe I couldn't accept myself as one of them.

When I moved back home to the Inland Empire after my father died, I started at a law firm in Riverside. It felt just as claustrophobic and soul-sapping as the firms in Houston and San Francisco. One day, a white male partner called me to remind me to wear a suit to a deposition. I raised my voice and retorted in a disapproving tone, "I know how and when to wear a suit" and hung up the phone. That night, I wondered to myself if that partner called his white male associates to remind them to dress professionally. The last straw was watching that same white male partner harshly criticize a female summer associate of color for not understanding a project. I stood up to him and advised the partner that I felt his tone was inappropriate. I yearned to flip him off, but held my fingers in check. This essay is my way of giving that partner the bird, Johnny Cash-style.

It was not until I attended a summer writing workshop called VONA (Voices of Our Nations Arts Foundation) and started writing creatively again that I found myself. Writing stories about my childhood and my teenage years made me remember who I was. It made me remember my blue collar background and upbringing. I started listening to all my favorite bands again and hanging out at the record stores—going to shows every weekend I could. Soon, I decided enough was enough and that my big firm law career was killing my soul. It was time to go.

I interviewed at multiple California public defender offices and the public defender's office in Riverside made me an offer right before a hiring freeze. In a twist of fate, the person who interviewed me and offered me the job was a supervisor named Brian who was a fan of punk rock and had seen the Sex Pistols live. When Brian called to offer me the deputy public defender job, I said yes on the spot, not caring that I was taking a huge financial hit. I took the leap and from my first day at the public defender's office I knew I had made the best decision of my life. I was finally home. Just writing about it makes me choke up.

Public defense is the opposite and the antithesis of corporate law. It is fighting the powers that be for your clients in a system that is stacked against them. At times, there is too much autonomy and not enough help or oversight or resources. But if you are a good lawyer, you make it work. If you love the underdog and a comeback story, you find your passion. For me, when I came back home, I finally found my purpose.

I still deal with stereotypes about what a lawyer looks like. Early in my public defense career, I walked into a trial courtroom and was told by a deputy sheriff that court was closed and only attorneys were allowed in. I explained that I was an attorney and walked inside. A few years ago, in trial court, a police officer asked if I was the interpreter. This had happened to me time and time again, and the misunderstanding was always made by white men. I looked at the young white police officer and said firmly, "I am Latina but do not speak Spanish. I am a USC Law-educated attorney and your assumptions are harmful." He took the education with grace.

My clients are a different story. They see themselves in me and my brown skin. One day, a colleague said, "Hey Juanita, a guy in custody is saying he is your cousin." I looked over and it turned out that the client in custody was, in fact, my cousin and my colleague found him a residential program and got him out of custody.

It probably helps that as a Latina lawyer, I am very assertive. I am also very responsive and always try to be kind to my clients and their families. From the outset I made a promise to myself that I would return every phone call timely. It's not always easy, but I get it done. My clients and their families respect me and are usually extremely grateful for my communication skills.

Despite the public perception of the public defense bar, I know firsthand that all of the coolest and hardest working lawyers are deputy public defenders. We don't do the job for the gold stars or a big paycheck, we do the job because we believe in justice for all, not just for some. We do the job because we care about those in our community that no one else cares about. We do the job because we want to fight "the man" and end a cruel system of injustice.

We fight for the most voiceless and oppressed. We go toe-to-toe with others in a system that is rigged. As a holdover from slavery and Jim Crow, the goal of the current criminal system is to incarcerate. The seminal book on this issue is *The New Jim Crow: Mass Incarceration in the Age of Color Blindness* by Michelle

Alexander.[17]

Even more horrific, the system is, at its core, racist and discriminates against the poor. As professor Angela Davis wrote in *Are Prisons Obsolete?*:[18]

> "Thus, if we are willing to take seriously the consequences of a racist and class based justice system, we will reach the conclusion that enormous numbers of people are in prison simply because they are, for example, black, Chicano, Vietnamese, Native American, or poor, regardless of their ethic background. They are sent to prison, not so much because of the crimes they may have indeed committed, but largely because their communities have been criminalized."

The system is stacked against people of color and the poor with Draconian laws and sentencing, unfair and discriminatory bail policies, and lack of treatment opportunities. It makes no sense. Salvation not incarceration should be the goal, but instead it is punishment and debilitation. At its core, the criminal system is inhumane, unjust, and unfair.

That is why it takes a punk rock rebel to fight against this unjust criminal system every day in her metaphorical combat boots, fist in the air.

---

17 *The New Jim Crow: Mass Incarceration in the Age of Colorblindness* by Michelle Alexander, The New Press (2010) & new edition (2020)

18 *Are Prisons Obsolete?* by Angela Y. Davis, Seven Stories Press (2003).

PRETTY VACANT: HOW OUR MENTAL HEALTH SYSTEM IS BROKEN

This morning I was thinking, my job is crazy, both literally and figuratively. By crazy, I mean chaotic for both me and my clients. I do not mean "crazy" pejoratively, but instead descriptively.

As I discussed earlier, I specialize in incompetency. It's a super technical and interesting field, but also constantly traumatizing as my clients are very mentally ill. My job is to navigate an impaired and disabled client through an impaired and broken system. It is not an easy job, but it is rewarding. Sometimes so rewarding, my eyes well up and tears almost spill out.

You would not believe the things I see. The only way to describe the courtroom I work in is this way: combine a goth version of *Alice in Wonderland* with *Law and Order*. Every day after walking my dogs, I go down the rabbit hole of incompetency, leaving my house thinking, "I'm late I'm late."

At the courthouse, some judges are like the Queen of Hearts, "Off with their heads!" But my current judge in mental health court is more benevolent. Yet, still, the courtroom I work in is a mad house tea party of sorts.

There are days when it is ridiculously crowded with clients in various states of mental illness, the vast majority of whom are in custody. Some are symptomatic and acting out by yelling. Other clients are crying. There are families in the audience who are distraught. It is utter, utter bedlam. My job is to give order to the chaos, to try and truly see and hear people, and offer some compassion, help, and advocacy.

My most important job is to be organized and kind. Nothing can fall through the cracks. It is a lot to juggle. The degree from USC Law helps, of course, as does my years of waitressing and learning how to multi-task and stay cool under pressure.

Our courtroom has none of the solemnity of a federal courthouse. It is state court all the way. Our current judge is a beacon of decorum, yet the things that happen are sometimes unbelievable.

Once, with our prior judge, there was a woman in the audience holding a cat puppet. The cat puppet had a top hat and a cane and the woman with the puppet was moving the puppet with the judge's voice. Watching and finally having enough, the deputy went over and told the woman, "Please put your cat puppet away." The woman did, stuffing the cat in her purse with a scowl and a "meow." I had to leave the courtroom after almost losing my composure.

Usually, most all of the time, my job is not funny, it is painful and just sad. So damn sad. The other day, I looked up from my seat at counsel table and said it aloud. I usually think it to myself numerous times a day, but that day, after seeing client after client in chains, I couldn't help myself and said, "This is so sad. Look at all of these poor people." The prosecutor on the other side of the table nodded taking a sip of her tea.

You see, we all know how bad, sad, and ineffectual our system is. We do. We see it every day. We see clients waiting hopelessly for beds that will never materialize, being warehoused in custody. The pandemic shattered what was an already broken system, but the problem is, these are lives and people. These people are someone's mother, someone's brother, someone's sister, son, and daughter.[19]

While the law is changing, it is a painful process, thick and slow like molasses, but a bitter one. Where do we put people that no one wants? Where do we put people that have done acts that are violent due to their mental illness? The truth is, no one wants my clients in their community. Patton State Hospital in

---

19 On June 15, 2021, in Stiavetti v. Clendenin, the California Court of Appeals (First Appellate District, Division Two) handed down a landmark decision in response to a class action brought by the ACLU on behalf of disabled, incompetent persons. In its ruling, the Court upheld an order that the state move incompetent to stand trial defendants into treatment facilities within days and not months, and set a strict schedule. As Justice J. Anthony Kline wrote, "Too many of these defendants' due process rights continue to be violated due to lengthy waits in county jails."

What is most crucial, is that the court system is FINALLY recognizing that the state is warehousing people with mental health and intellectual disabilities, rather than treating them, and that the horror of that is substantial and real, and now, it's finally out in the open.

San Bernardino has been there for over a hundred years and ironically, abuts the San Manuel Casino. No one wants a board and care or a residential rehab in their nice community. We all want the problem to go away without having to see it firsthand, much less next door.

I saw a movie recently called *Clemency* and in it, a man is on death row. All of the people involved suffer by participating in the system. The warden suffers, the defense attorney suffers, and most of all, the condemned client suffers. This broken down system of injustice impacts all who work in it. My point is, through this punishing and inhuman model we use, we are inflicting suffering on humans which, in turn, harms those who participate in it.

We lawyers who work in the trenches day in and day out have to remember we are warriors and work hard to stay passionate with our eyes wide open to the suffering around us and not become desensitized to people in chains. We must work hard to always see the tragic system we work in and our clients. We must tell our client's stories and our own. Most of all, we must work hard to not let the criminal system program us.

The criminal system is a surreal and chaotic ride. For now, I just go to work every day. I don't call in sick. My clients need me. And yes, it's true, I need them.

HOW A NOT-SO-SWEET HOOLIGAN GIRL ESCAPED INCARCERATION

I was a juvenile delinquent as a kid in different times. I ditched school (what would be called chronic truancy in these times), vandalized property, dined and dashed, shoplifted, drank in public, got into fights[20], stole my father's car (in violation of the current CA Penal Code section 10851, but the statute of limitations has long passed), and drove without a driver's license and insurance on many occasions.

In my senior year of high school, my parents left for the weekend and I threw a kegger party, meaning I "borrowed" kegs from the pizza place where I worked, had them filled, and charged people

---

[20] I was and am an inept fighter. My first fight resulted in me getting my ass kicked and the second time, my twin sister fought for me by proxy. My opponent was a heavy set chola who wore her hair straight up, blow-dried with Aqua-Net. She told me to meet her in South Quad after school to fight. Word got around quick and my twin sister Jackie ran up to me at lunch. Jackie looked at me and said, "You can't fight her, that girl is tough. She'll kick your ass." Jackie lectured me, "Dammit, why do you always have to talk shit if you can't back it up?" My eyes watered and I said, "I know," with a sigh. Jackie hesitated, shrugged her shoulders and said, "Fuck it, I'll fight her for you." I remember them going at it, blow after blow, for what seemed like twelve rounds. Jackie totally held her own and the fight was unofficially called a draw. Jackie saved me a serious ass-kicking that day.

to come in and drink beer. The police came and I told them off. I was not arrested.

Is it that times were different when I grew up? Or perhaps I was just lucky, or privileged? I think it is all three. Back in the '80s, if you were caught shoplifting, the store usually called your parents. That happened to me more than once. And when I was fourteen or so, I used to steal my dad's truck at night when he was asleep and drive through the streets of Upland on a lark. One night, my dad woke up to find me and his truck missing and called the police. My dad called the police because he was worried, not because he wanted me arrested. The cops brought me home. I slept in my own bed that night.

When I was ticketed for drinking in public in the condos that we lived for a time in Upland, my punishment was to attend a "Just Say No" set of alcoholism classes. I was never taken into any kind of system or court that I can recall. I don't even remember my parents being involved.

My custody time has been very brief. At nineteen, I was arrested for shoplifting and given a cite release and sentenced to a very large fine of hundreds of dollars that I paid off in twenty dollar increments with my waitressing tips. I more than learned my lesson. Then later, after throwing away a jaywalking ticket, I was taken to jail on the warrant after being pulled over. My boyfriend at the time, who is now my husband, bailed me out of the arguably cushy La Verne jail where the cops ordered a pizza and treated me like a human being.

I dropped out of high school. Yet, after working my way through junior college and UC Riverside, I ended up at USC Law. Upon graduation and upon passing the bar exam, I wrote an essay detailing my shoplifting ticket which had been expunged by that time and my jaywalking in custody experience and was quickly admitted as a lawyer, despite my decades old moral failings.

My clients are not so lucky.

What many people don't realize is that less supervision is better in most situations. Allowing a kid to make a mistake, and not having it be fatal, is crucial. Discipline and an iron fist only makes a kid pull at the yoke and encourages them to rebel and fight. Less police presence (i.e., no cops on school grounds) is key. In my high school, we only had inept proctors who policed smoking ineffectively. Fights typically weren't prosecuted or even discovered.

I guess what I am here to say is this: give kids a chance to grow and learn what's right and sometimes that's best taught by allowing them to do wrong.

When I am in court, I always think to myself, that person in chains could be me or a family member or friend. Maybe all of us need to realize that, but for luck or circumstances, that person in chains could be us.

Bail - How Times Are A-Changin'

All my clients are very poor, otherwise known as indigent. I get much more satisfaction from representing the poor and oppressed than I ever did when I represented large corporations.

Most of my indigent clientele are in custody. Although I am now assigned to handling incompetency proceedings under PC section 1368, I spent years handling felony preliminary hearings and trials in the general felony courtroom as well as years in Drug Court. I spent sixteen months working in the Banning courthouse, which serves a very low income community, before that. In my tenure in those departments, I saw client after client plead guilty in order to get out of custody.

The ultimate act of state sponsored coercion is bail. These bail policies are further evidence of the systemic goal of incarceration because when bail is the rule, then the result is incarceration unless you have enough money to bail out. I would argue that the mere setting of bail is a discriminatory and coercive act, designed to incarcerate and force people to plead guilty.

Some have addressed the concept of bail in a criminal case and whether it is right and just as well as the many detriments of cash bail and why statistically it doesn't make sense.[21] A study also came

21 "The Case Against Cash Bail," *The New Yorker* by Margaret Talbot, August 25, 2015; "The Collateral Victims of Criminal Justice," *The New York Times* by Shaila Dewan, September 5, 2015.

out in 2013 detailing how bail and pretrial detention actually results in an increased rate of recidivism and uncovered strong correlations between the length of time low- and moderate-risk offenders were detained before trial and the likelihood that they would reoffend in both the short and long term.[22]

Regardless, I have seen it firsthand. Bail ruins lives and causes innocent people to plead guilty to avoid staying incarcerated.[23]

If all of these criminal procedures regarding bail seem counterproductive, they are. There is another option that is rarely used in felony cases called a release on "OR" which stands for a release on one's "own recognizance" which allows a criminal defendant to be released on their own promise to appear. It is rarely used in felony cases, however, to many of my clients' detriment.

This may have all changed due to a California Supreme Court case ruling that was just issued this year on March 25, 2021. In the case *In Re Humphrey,* the California Supreme Court ruled

---

22 "The Hidden Costs of Pretrial Detention" by Christopher T. Lowenkamp, Ph.D., Marie Vannostrand Ph.D., and Alexander Holsinger, Ph.D., (November 2013).

23 "The Case Against Cash Bail", *The New Yorker* by Margaret Talbot, August 25, 2015; "The Collateral Victims of Criminal Justice", *The New York Times* by Shaila Dewan, September 5, 2015.

that bail for the indigent may indeed be unconstitutional.[24] The case was pretty simple, an elderly man followed a neighbor into his apartment in their senior citizen community and took seven dollars and a bottle of cologne. The man's bail was set at $600,000 dollars, more than half a million dollars, due to his prior strike convictions. Then, after his attorney's zealous advocacy, it was lowered to $350,000. This extremely high bail was set despite the fact that the man was indigent, and despite the fact that his strikes were decades old. His attorney, who did everything right, said his client could not afford such high bail and that he had secured a drug rehabilitation program for the elderly client and thus, the risk to public safety was low. The defense attorney filed a writ challenging the $350,000 bail and the California Supreme Court found that the setting of bail at that amount was unconstitutional stating,

> "Yet if a court does not consider an arrestee's ability to pay, it cannot know whether requiring money bail in a particular amount is likely to operate as the functional equivalent of a pretrial detention order. Detaining an arrestee in such circumstances accords insufficient respect to the arrestee's crucial state and federal equal protection rights against wealth-based detention as well as the ar-

---

24 IN THE SUPREME COURT OF CALIFORNIA, *In re KENNETH HUMPHREY on Habeas Corpus*, S247278, First Appellate District, Division Two A152056 San Francisco City and County Superior Court 17007715, March 25, 2021.

restee's state and federal substantive due process rights to pretrial liberty."

What the Court is saying here, and in the rest of its opinion, is that bail is wrong, unjust, unfair, and ultimately, discriminatory and the taking away of someone's liberty should not be taken lightly and perhaps, as I have argued here, that incarceration should be a last resort.

Hopefully, times may be a-changing. The reason I say things "may be" changing is that, like all court rulings, the new bail ruling must be put into practice. Thus, it will be up to us as criminal defense attorneys to fight like hell for judges to enforce this new ruling and get our clients released without having to post bail. The problem is that we have created an incarcerated class in America and that is most true here in the Inland Empire.

Where I practice in Riverside, incarceration is typically the default. We incarcerate and create bail schedules because for those in power it is easier than doing a case-by-case analysis. The practice of incarceration is made plain by the bail amount shown on each complaint.

It cannot be denied that the practice of bail is discriminatory. We all know this. It's obvious. Bail says if you have the money you can go home. If not, stay incarcerated until you prove your innocence. This is pretrial. Pretrial, meaning these people have not been convicted of anything. Not convicted YET, some may say. But that is the worst kind of analysis because we have a presumption of innocence in the United States of America, supposed land of the free and the brave. Thus, you must assume these people in the courtroom, that these people—not defendants, not bodies[25], but people—are innocent.

Finally, let me offer you an allegory for why bail doesn't make sense. Imagine twin brothers charged with the same crime, one is rich, one is poor. They are similar, except of course for their bank accounts. Imagine they are arrested on two separate, but almost identical cases. Imagine their bail is each set at fifty-thousand dollars (which usually requires at least five to ten percent cash down to the bail bonds company and monthly payments).

Now, imagine that the brothers are estranged and only the "rich man" has the money to pay to bail out. Imagine someone without money, resources, education, or friends and family much less a credit card and/or a bank account.

What should the "poor man" do? Would you sit in custody and wait for trial?

Next, imagine the poor man is offered a deal by his deputy public defender, an attorney who sincerely cares when her client says he is innocent and/or that he has a defense of self-defense, but who also has the duty to convey all offers. The District Attorney is offering the poor man 180 days on work release and a strike

---

25 In the ultimate act of utter dehumanization, the deputies call our incarcerated clients "bodies". They will say, "Bring the bodies up to court."

felony with formal probation for three years. That deal lets the poor man go home. The poor man knows he has a defense but he also knows he has a kid at home that needs to be looked after, and pets and a job he will lose if he stays incarcerated. What would you do? Now imagine we are in a pandemic and the man's very life is at risk in custody.

We all know what happens. The poor man pleads guilty and is stuck with a felony with three years minimum of felony probation and a strike, and the rich man stays out of custody and eventually gets a misdemeanor on the day of trial. The poor man eventually violates probation for not doing his work release because he couldn't miss work and is sent to prison. **The poor man eventually ends up losing everything he tried so hard not to lose.**

The most pressing question still remains. If we have a presumption of innocence in America, why do we have bail at all? Or maybe the presumption of innocence is, in all practicality, in form only because we know that in real life, money talks when it comes to pretrial detention. Just ask the poor man.

If the truth be told, I hope the *In Re Humphrey* decision means everything.[26] Yet, I also know that the fear that comes along

---

26 Regardless of what happens in California, remember that bail is the norm in most of the United States so we must continue to fight for the rest of the country to change their inhumane and discriminatory bail practices in which incarceration is the default.

with doing the right thing is intense. It requires judges who are not scared to follow the law and attorneys who are diligent and invested to raise the bail issue and fight it on every case where it demands a fight. We shall have to wait and see what happens.

That said, I remain optimistic and know that I must speak out for change. When I first started writing this book, I thought I might be called out for saying the truth. Then I thought, what is freedom for if not to speak out for those who are not free? So speak out I must, and I will raise the issues on the micro level on my cases, but I am here on the macro level to say, let's do the right thing.

The right thing is hard. It requires work, diligence and courage. Most of all, doing the right and just thing requires us all to work together for change to make this criminal system fairer and much more equitable. It can't come fast enough.

WHO AM I?

Torn in pieces
A deputy public defender
Who knows I am
Participating in a
Broken system

In tatters, shattered
Eyes wide open
No one would believe
What I see
What I have seen

It's not my trauma
Or maybe it is
Carrying it
For the poor
Oppressed

Selective enforcement
All too real
In their cages
Clients beg
To be heard

The State sanctioned
Brutality of
Mass incarceration
Carries on with
Its own momentum

Where do I go
What do I do
When I don't believe
In reformation
Abolition the only answer

These are people
Can't you see
Those in power
Ignored our cries
For far too long

There is a higher law
I always knew it
In my soul
Just "say no" they said
Now weed is legal

How easy to judge
Prosecutors' glass houses
Well comfortable
No more
No more I say

Your walls are shattered
Broken glass everywhere
Help us
Please help us
Rebuild

About the Author

Juanita E. Mantz ("JEM") is a deputy public defender, writer, performer and podcaster, one who believes that stories have the power to change the world. She graduated from UCR in 1999 with a Bachelor's in English Literature and received her J.D. from USC Law in 2002. She is in the low residency MFA creative writing program at The University of New Orleans.

Juanita has been with the Law Offices of the Public Defender in Riverside County for over a decade. She specializes in representing incompetent clients under PC Section 1368 and has taken many serious felony cases to trial on the mental health issues.

Juanita is an alumna of VONA and The Macondo Writers Workshop and serves on the Board of Directors of the Inlandia Institute. She has been published widely, including in *The Acentos Review, Aljazeera, As/Us, Bitch Media, The Dirty Spoon, Entropy, Inlandia, The James Franco Review, MUSE, Riverside Press Enterprise*, and the *San Bernardino-Singing* (anthology), amongst others. She performed in the 2016 cast of *Listen to Your Mother,* Burbank. She has presented at the UCR Punk Conference, AWP and Beyond Baroque. She also produced and taught in the ASA 2020 Freedom Course on Combatting Mass Incarceration.

On her video "Life of JEM" podcast, she does live interviews with artists, wellness practitioners and writers. You can find everything on her author website: https://juanitaemantz.com.

BAMBOO
DART
PRESS

112 N. Harvard Ave. #65
Claremont, CA 91711

chapbooks@bamboodartpress.com
www.bamboodartpress.com

* 9 7 8 1 9 4 7 2 4 0 3 0 8 *